Contents

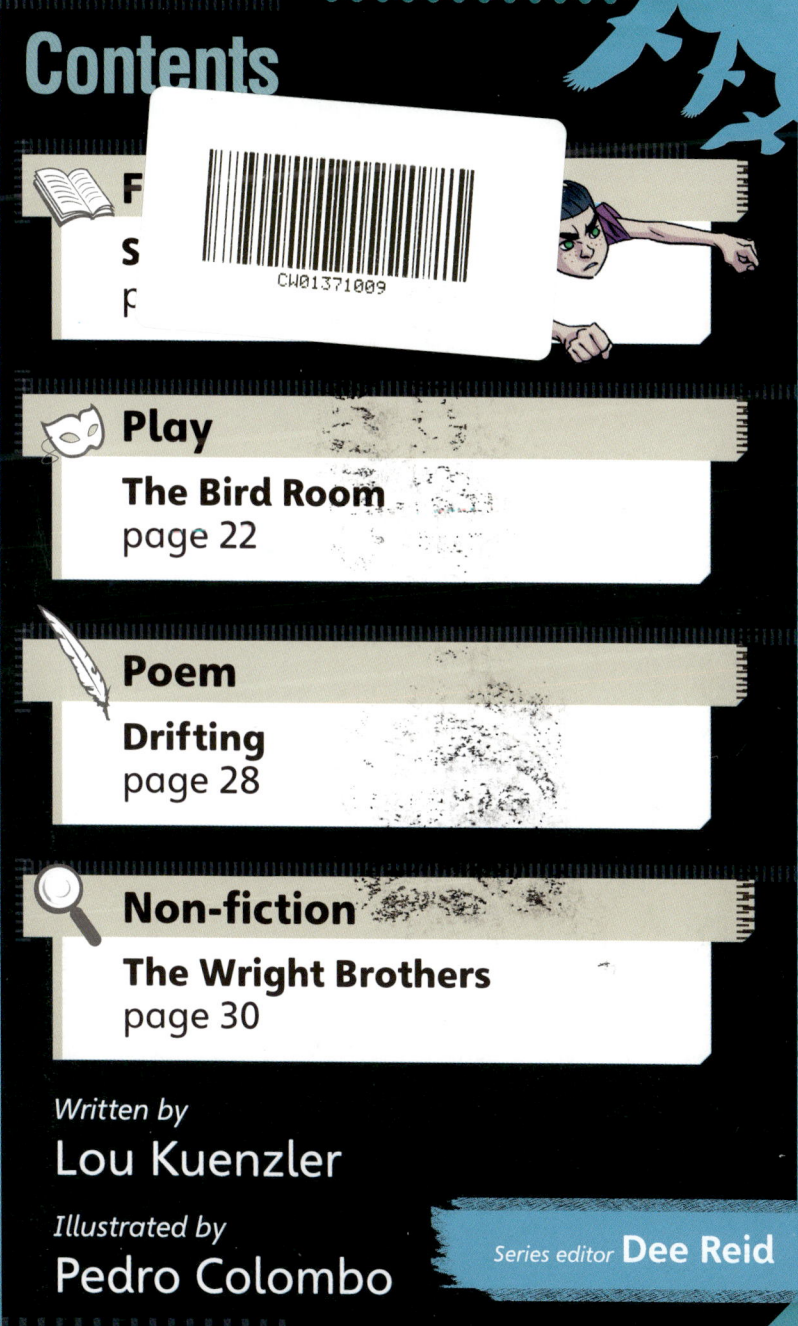

F
S
p

Play
The Bird Room
page 22

Poem
Drifting
page 28

Non-fiction
The Wright Brothers
page 30

Written by
Lou Kuenzler

Illustrated by
Pedro Colombo

Series editor **Dee Reid**

Before reading
Sky Boy

Characters

Rory

Meg

Dr Wilde

Scorpion

Tricky words

ch1 p3	Aquarium
ch1 p3	Museum
ch1 p5	fascinated
ch1 p5	Awesome
ch1 p6	familiar
ch2 p9	ceiling
ch2 p9	muscles
ch3 p15	distance

Story starter

When Rory and his sister, Meg, breathed in a strange gas in Dr Wilde's lab, they developed super powers. Rory can fly like a bird and Meg can breathe under water. Now evil Dr Wilde wants to catch them to find out how their super powers work. One day, Rory and Meg went to London. Rory visited the Natural History Museum and Meg went to the London Aquarium.

Sky Boy

Chapter One

Meg and I were in London for the day. We thought the busy city would be a good place to hide from evil Dr Wilde. Meg said she wanted to see the sharks at the London Aquarium. I wanted to visit the Natural History Museum. We agreed to meet up later by the river next to Big Ben.

I spent ages in the museum. The best bit was the room full of stuffed birds. They had interesting diagrams to show how wing shapes help different birds to stay in the air.

Ever since I found out I could fly, I have been fascinated by birds. I stared up at a golden eagle. Its wings were spread like the wings of a fighter jet. *Awesome!* I thought.

Suddenly my phone rang. It was Meg. "You're late," she snapped. "You were supposed to meet me ten minutes ago." I looked at my watch. "Sorry Meg!" I cried. "I will meet you by Big Ben as soon as I can."

"So, Rory, you plan to meet your sister at Big Ben. How interesting," said a familiar voice behind me.
A shiver ran down my spine.

Chapter Two

I slipped the phone into my pocket as Dr Wilde grabbed my arm.
"Get off!" I cried, dodging sideways.
There was a man with her. He had a tattoo of a scorpion on his cheek.
"You can't escape," he said.

I looked around for help but Dr Wilde and her henchman must have waited until the bird room was empty.
"There is no way you can fly out of here," sneered Dr Wilde, pointing a red fingernail around the room.

Dr Wilde was wrong. I looked up at the high ceiling. She had not noticed the small open skylight high above me. I felt my muscles tense and I rose into the air like an eagle.

"You can't catch me!" I cried.
"Grab him, Scorpion!" screeched Dr Wilde.
Scorpion's fingers clutched at me like claws, but I was too quick for him.
I shot up towards the skylight.

"Never mind, I will catch your sister instead!" said Dr Wilde. "She can show me how to breathe under water!"
She laughed an evil laugh.

Then Dr Wilde turned to Scorpion. "Bring my motorbike to the front door!" she shouted. "The boy has escaped, but I will catch his sister. I will ride to Big Ben."

Chapter Three

I looked down from high up above the museum. I saw Dr Wilde jumping onto a yellow motorbike.
I must warn Meg before Dr Wilde can catch her! I thought. I grabbed for my phone, but it slipped through my fingers and fell out of sight.

Come on! I told myself, speeding through the air. *I need to go quicker than Dr Wilde's motorbike! I must get to Big Ben and find Meg before she does.* The trouble was, I had never been to London before. I had no idea where Big Ben was.

I flew higher to get a better look.
I saw some grey water in the distance.
That is the river! I thought. *Meg said Big Ben was by the river!*
Just then, I saw the yellow motorbike racing along below me.

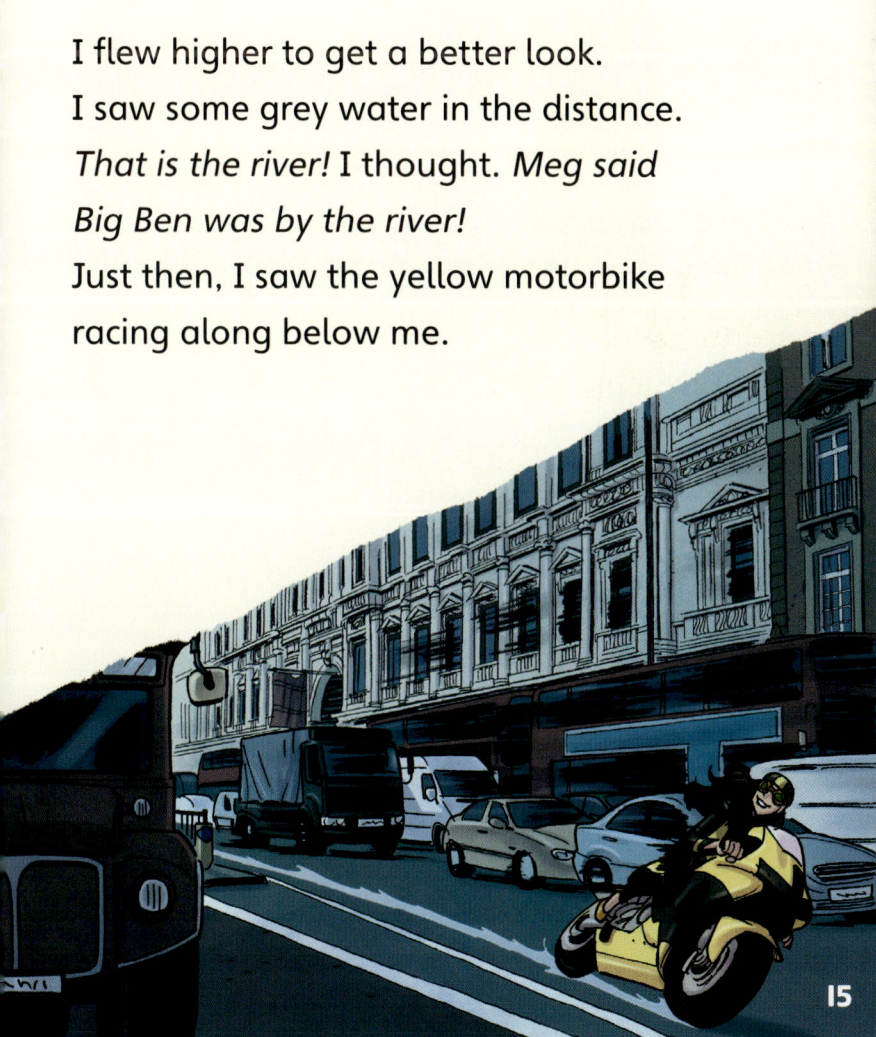

Chapter Four

"There it is!" I cried as I flew towards the river. Ahead of me I could see the tall clock of Big Ben. I scanned the streets below me. *Good*, I thought, *no sign of the yellow motorbike*. I had got there first.

I swooped into an empty alleyway and landed where nobody could see me. I began to run as soon as my feet hit the ground. I spotted Meg leaning on the railings by the river. Then I saw Dr Wilde. She was racing towards Meg on foot.

"Look out!" I cried. I sprang forward.
Dr Wilde grabbed Meg's arm.
"Let her go!" I shouted.
Meg pulled herself free. Dr Wilde spun round and caught me instead.
"Got you!" she screeched.
"Run, Rory!" cried Meg, stamping on Dr Wilde's foot.

I pulled my arm free and Meg and I
sprinted along the edge of the river.
"Jump!" said Meg, grabbing my hand.
We jumped into the freezing grey
water below.
"Get on my back!" said Meg.
She swam along like a seal
below the surface.

Within seconds we were on the opposite bank of the river. We could see Dr Wilde shaking her fist at us.

"Quick! In here," I said as we dashed into a café where we could get warm and dry. We had escaped … for now.

Quiz

Text detective

- **p3** Why do you think Meg was interested in seeing the sharks?
- **p10** How did Rory escape from Dr Wilde in the Natural History Museum?
- **p13** Why couldn't Rory warn Meg?
- **p17** Why do you think Rory landed where nobody could see him?
- **p20** Why did Dr Wilde shake her fist at Rory and Meg?

Word detective

- **p5** Find a simile. Explain why you think comparing these two things is effective.
- **p17** Which verb reminds you that Rory can fly like a bird?

What do you think?

Dr Wilde is determined to catch Rory. What do you think she would do if she caught Rory or Meg?

HA! HA!

Q: What do you call a sick eagle?

A: Ill-eagle!

Before reading
The Bird Room

Characters

- **Dr Wilde** – a scientist
- **Scorpion** – Dr Wilde's henchman
- **Rory** – a boy with the power to fly

Setting the scene

Evil scientist Dr Wilde and her henchman, Scorpion, have secretly followed Rory into the Bird Room of the Natural History Museum. Dr Wilde is determined to catch Rory and take him to her lab to find out how his super power works.

The Bird Room

Rory: Wow! A golden eagle! It looks just like a fighter jet.

Scorpion: *(whispering)* Is that the boy we are going to catch?

Dr Wilde: Yes. That is the boy.

Scorpion: He doesn't look like he can fly like a bird. How is he able to fly?

Dr Wilde: There was an explosion in my lab.

Scorpion: An explosion?

Dr Wilde: Yes. A strange gas escaped. The boy and his sister breathed in the gas. It gave them special powers.

Scorpion: And that is why the boy can fly?

Dr Wilde: Yes … and his sister can breathe under water.

Scorpion: Wow! So why are we going to catch them?

Dr Wilde: You fool, Scorpion! I am going to experiment on them. I have to know how their powers work so I can use them for myself.

(Rory's phone rings.)

Rory: Hello. Meg?

Dr Wilde: That is his sister on the phone!

Rory: Sorry, Meg. I didn't notice the time.

Scorpion: I will grab him now.

Dr Wilde: Wait. He might say where his sister is.

Rory: I will meet you by Big Ben as soon as I can.

Dr Wilde: So, Rory, you plan to meet your sister at Big Ben. How interesting. Now I know where to find you *and* your sister.

Rory: Get away from me!

Dr Wilde: I have come to take you to my lab.

Scorpion: She is going to put you in a cage and experiment on you.

Dr Wilde: I will find out how your powers work. Then I will use them for myself.

Rory: You will have to catch me first!

Scorpion: You can't escape.

Dr Wilde: There is no way you can fly out of here.

Rory: That's where you are wrong! There is a skylight!

(Rory takes off.)

Dr Wilde: Grab him, Scorpion! He is getting away.

Rory: You can't catch me!

Dr Wilde: Never mind, I will catch your sister instead! She can show me how to breathe under water!

Quiz

Play detective

p23	How is Rory able to fly?
p23	Find a word for a building used for scientific experiments.
p24–25	Why does Dr Wilde want to know where Meg is?
p25–26	What evidence is there that Dr Wilde is evil?
p27	What does Rory say that shows he is confident he will get away?

Before reading
Drifting

Setting the scene

Have you ever seen anything fluttering in the breeze? The poem describes what it is like to drift in the breeze. It is told in the first person.

Poem top tip

In verse 2, look out for a clue that helps you work out who the speaker is. In verse 3, pause after the word 'fall' in the last line to emphasise the surprise ending.

Quiz

Poem detective

- Who is the speaker?
- Why does the plastic bag fall to the ground?
- How has the poet made a plastic bag sound interesting?
- Find examples of alliteration. What effect does it have?

Drifting

Drifting on a gentle breeze,
I flap and flutter in the trees.
Drifting in a circle there,
I flutter and flap in the air.

Drifting on the gentle breeze,
I flutter and flap in the trees.
Fluttering my plastic wings,
I flap in circles, drift in rings.

The gentle drifting breeze is gone.
I cannot drift and flutter on.
My plastic wings flap and sag,
I fall … a fluttering plastic bag.

by Lou Kuenzler

Before reading
The Wright Brothers

Find out about

- Orville and Wilbur Wright and their determination to fly
- How they built the first plane
- How they used a bicycle to get the plane moving.

Tricky words

p32	enough	p35	decided
p33	machines	p36	distance
p34	propellers	p38	Typhoon

Text starter

Orville and Wilbur Wright were brothers who were very interested in flying. They owned a bicycle shop and began to understand how machines worked. Their first plane had wings, propellers, an engine and rudders for steering. At first their attempts failed but in 1903 their plane flew.

The Wright Brothers

The toy

When Orville Wright was 7 years old and his brother Wilbur was 11, their father gave them a toy that could fly. It had an elastic band to power it. The toy soon broke, but it made the brothers want to fly for real. That toy changed history.

Wilbur read a lot about how birds fly. He wanted wings of his own to fly.

Orville sold kites at school to make money. He wanted to make a kite strong enough to lift a person.

After a lot of attempts, Orville built some gliders that were strong enough to lift a person off the ground, but they always crashed.

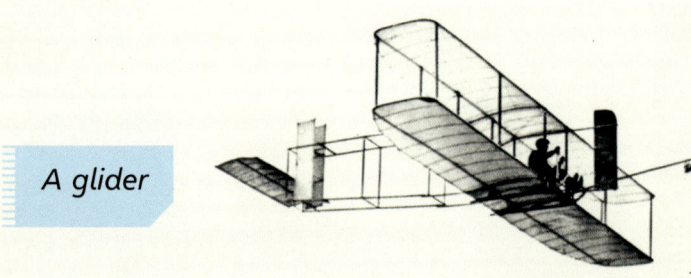

A glider

When the brothers grew up, Orville and Wilbur owned a bicycle shop.

They began to understand how machines worked.

Orville and Wilbur wanted to build a real plane. The plane needed:

- wings that could lift it off the ground
- an engine that could propel it along
- a way of steering it when it was flying.

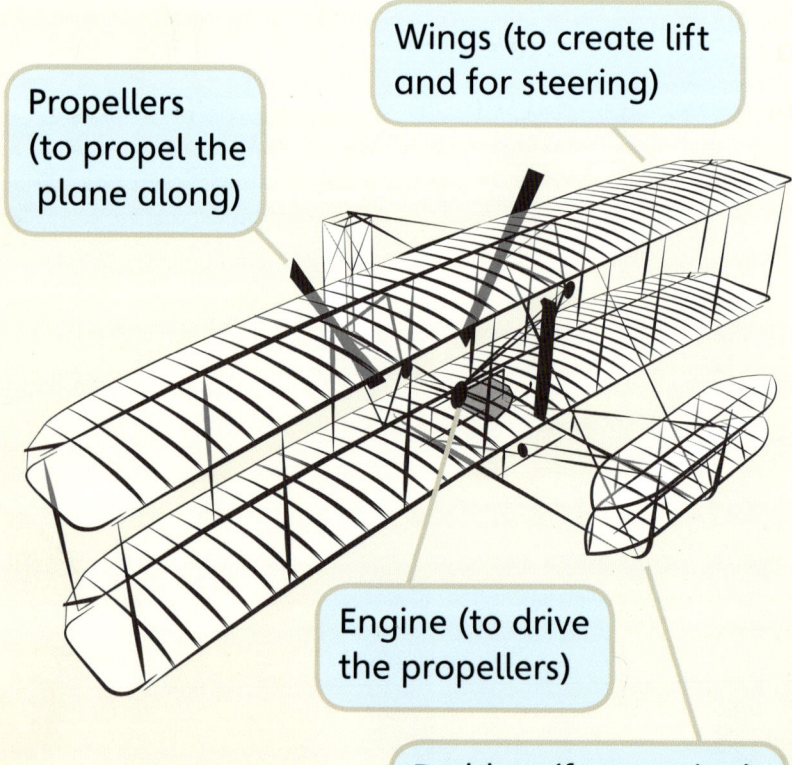

Wings (to create lift and for steering)

Propellers (to propel the plane along)

Engine (to drive the propellers)

Rudders (for steering)

The biggest problem was how to steer the plane. Orville had noticed that birds twist their wings to change direction. The brothers decided to build a plane that could twist its wings. Then they could steer the plane when it was flying.

The brothers decided that Wilbur would fly the plane first. Orville had to push the plane down a hill for it to take off. The plane crashed. The brothers decided the hill was too steep.

A Great Day for Flight: 17th December 1903

Next they tried to take off from flatter ground. Now Wilbur had to push the plane along and Orville had to pedal the plane like a bicycle.

The plane did not fly for a long time, and it did not fly a long distance, but it did fly.

Flight time	Distance
12 seconds	37 m

It was official! The Wright brothers had built a plane that could fly.

Modern planes

Flight has come a long way since the Wright brothers. A modern plane like the Typhoon jet can fly at twice the speed of sound. Imagine how Orville and Wilbur would feel if they could fly a modern jet!

Quiz

Text detective

- **p31** What first made the Wright brothers interested in flying?
- **p35** What was the biggest problem they faced?
- **p35** How did the brothers work as a team?
- **p38** What are some differences between the Wright brothers' plane and modern jets?

Non-fiction features

- **p33** Think of a caption for this picture.
- **p34** How does the layout of this page help you to understand how the first plane worked?

What do you think?

Can you think of a new form of transport that you would like to create? What would be good about it?

HA! HA!

Q: What's the difference between a plane and a tree?

A: One leaves its shed and the other sheds its leaves!

Published by Pearson Education Limited, a company incorporated in England and Wales, having its registered office at Edinburgh Gate, Harlow, Essex, CM20 2JE.
Registered company number: 872828

www.pearsonschools.co.uk

Pearson is a registered trademark of Pearson plc

Text © Pearson Education Limited 2013

The right of Lou Kuenzler to be identified as the author of this work has been asserted by her in accordance with the Copyright, Designs and Patents Act 1988.

First published 2013

18 17 16 15 14 13
10 9 8 7 6 5 4 3 2 1

British Library Cataloguing in Publication Data is available from the British Library on request.

ISBN: 978 0 435 15232 1

Copyright notice
All rights reserved. No part of this publication may be reproduced in any form or by any means (including photocopying or storing it in any medium by electronic means and whether or not transiently or incidentally to some other use of this publication) without the written permission of the copyright owner, except in accordance with the provisions of the Copyright, Designs and Patents Act 1988 or under the terms of a licence issued by the Copyright Licensing agency, Saffron House, 6-10 Kirby Street, London EC1N 8TS (www.cla.co.uk). Applications for the copyright owner's written permission should be addressed to the publisher.

Designed by Bigtop
Original illustrations © Pearson Education Limited 2013
Cover, fiction and play illustrated by Pedro Colombo
Diagram on page 34 illustrated by Darren Lingard
Printed and bound in Malaysia (CTP-VP)
Font © Pearson Education Ltd
Teaching notes by Dee Reid

Acknowledgements
We would like to thank the following schools for their invaluable help in the development and trialling of this course:

Callicroft Primary School, Bristol; Castlehill Primary School, Fife; Elmlea Junior School, Bristol; Lancaster School, Essex; Llanidloes School, Powys; Moulton School, Newmarket; Platt C of E Primary School, Kent; Sherborne Abbey CE VC Primary School, Dorset; Upton Junior School, Poole; Whitmore Park School, Coventry.

The author and publisher would like to thank the following individuals and organisations for permission to reproduce photographs:

(Key: b-bottom; c-centre; l-left; r-right; t-top)
Alamy Images: GL Archive 32b, LOC Photo 36–37b, RGB Ventures LLC dba SuperStock 33b; **DK Images:** Peter Dennis 31b; **Shutterstock.com:** PJF 38b

All other images © Pearson Education

Every effort has been made to contact copyright holders of material reproduced in this book. Any omissions will be rectified in subsequent printings if notice is given to the publishers.